Zendaya

By Robin Johnson

CRABTREE
PUBLISHING COMPANY
WWW.CRABTREEBOOKS.COM

CRABTREE
PUBLISHING COMPANY
WWW.CRABTREEBOOKS.COM

Author: Robin Johnson

Editor: Kathy Middleton

Proofreaders: Lorna Notsch, Crystal Sikkens

Photo research: Ken Wright, Robin Johnson

Design and prepress: Ken Wright

Print coordinator: Katherine Berti

Every effort has been made to trace copyright holders and to obtain their permission for use of copyright material. The authors and publishers would be pleased to rectify any error or omission in future editions. All the Internet addresses given in this book were correct at the time of going to press. The author and publishers regret any inconvenience caused if addresses have changed or sites have ceased to exist, but can accept no responsibility for any such changes.

Photo Credits

Alamy: p 6, The Photo Access; p 10, ZUMA Press, Inc.; pp 13, 22, WENN Ltd; p 19, PA Images; p 25, Moviestore collection Ltd; p 26, © Birdie Thompson/AdMedia via ZUMA Wire; p 28, mjmediabox / Alamy Live News

Getty: p 7, Alberto E. Rodriguez; p 8, Earl Gibson III; p 12, Disney Channel / Contributor; p 16, ©Bob D'Amico/Disney ABC Television Group; p 17, ©Tony Rivetti/Disney ABC Television Group; p 18, David Livingston

Keystone: front cover, © wenn.com;

Shutterstock: title page, pp 4, 9, 15, 20, Kathy Hutchins; p 5, Sky Cinema; p 11, Featureflash Photo Agency; P 14, Jaguar PS; p 21, s_bukley; pp 23, 24, Tinseltown; p 27, Phil Stafford

Library and Archives Canada Cataloguing in Publication

Johnson, Robin (Robin R.), author
    Zendaya / Robin Johnson.

(Superstars!)
Includes index.
Issued in print and electronic formats.
ISBN 978-0-7787-4843-4 (hardcover).--
ISBN 978-0-7787-4872-4 (softcover).--
ISBN 978-1-4271-2099-1 (HTML)

    1. Zendaya, 1996- --Juvenile literature. 2. Television actors and actresses--United States--Biography--Juvenile literature. 3. Models (Persons)--Biography--Juvenile literature. 4. Singers--United States--Biography--Juvenile literature. 5. Motion picture actors and actresses--United States--Biography--Juvenile literature. I. Title. I. Series: Superstars! (St. Catharines, Ont.)

PN2287.Z47J46 2018   j791.4502'8092   C2018-900285-9
                                        C2018-900286-7

Library of Congress Cataloging-in-Publication Data

Names: Johnson, Robin, author.
Title: Zendaya / Robin Johnson.
Description: New York : Crabtree Publishing, [2018] | Series: Superstars! | Includes index.
Identifiers: LCCN 2018005823 (print) | LCCN 2018007417 (ebook) | ISBN 9781427120991 (Electronic) | ISBN 9780778748434 (hardcover) | ISBN 9780778748724 (pbk.)
Subjects: LCSH: Zendaya, 1996---Juvenile literature. | Actors--United States--Biography--Juvenile literature. | Singers--United States--Biography--Juvenile literature. | Models (Persons)--United States--Biography--Juvenile literature.
Classification: LCC PN2287.Z47 (ebook) | LCC PN2287.Z47 J64 2018 (print) | DDC 791.4302/8092 [B] --dc23
LC record available at https://lccn.loc.gov/2018005823

Crabtree Publishing Company
www.crabtreebooks.com   1-800-387-7650

Printed in the U.S.A./052018/BG20180327

Published in Canada
Crabtree Publishing
616 Welland Ave.
St. Catharines, ON
L2M 5V6

Published in the United States
Crabtree Publishing
PMB 59051
350 Fifth Avenue, 59th Floor
New York, New York 10118

Published in the United Kingdom
Crabtree Publishing
Maritime House
Basin Road North, Hove
BN41 1WR

Published in Australia
Crabtree Publishing
3 Charles Street
Coburg North
VIC 3058

CONTENTS

Words that are defined in the glossary are in
bold type the first time they appear in the text.

Supergirl

Zendaya is a Disney darling who started shaking things up on TV at a young age. But—as the **outspoken** actor often reminds her many fans—no one is ever just one thing. Zendaya is a talented singer and dancer. She is a focused, ambitious businessperson who knows what she wants and is not afraid to go after it. She is a natural cover girl and a style star with her own fashion line. She is a vocal **activist** who promotes respect and encourages others to use their voice.

Rise to Fame

Zendaya became an overnight sensation when she was just 14. The young actor rose to fame playing Rocky Blue on the Disney Channel show *Shake It Up*. She went on to star in the TV movies *Frenemies* and *Zapped*. She later released an album, danced with the stars, and even wrote a book—all before the age of 18. Then she returned to Disney as a teenage spy on the popular series *K.C. Undercover*. Zendaya recently hit the big screen, appearing in the feature films *Spider-Man: Homecoming* and *The Greatest Showman*.

Zendaya is a **role model** for young people all around the world.

4

Fashion Is Her Kryptonite

As an actor, Zendaya plays different roles, but she is also known for transforming herself with her unique fashion choices. The stylish superstar loves to shake things up with her "fashion-fierce" looks. The five-foot-ten-inch (1.8-m) tall, hazel-eyed beauty is constantly pushing the limits of fashion. Her daring looks turn heads—and often make headlines! But Zendaya chooses her outfits and hairstyles with care. She tries to be a representative for different types of beauty.

As she says in her song "Fashion Is My Kryptonite," Zendaya's got style in her veins and fashion in her blood.

66 She Said It 99

"I get to represent a lot of different types of women because of my ability to transform into these different people. I think a lot of women can see themselves in me and a lot of people in general are empowered by seeing someone wear what they want, do what they want…"
—Interview in *Elle,* November 2016

Girl Power

Zendaya is a powerful role model for young women everywhere. The social media star has more than 49 million followers on Instagram and 13 million followers on Twitter. She understands the responsibility of having such a huge social media platform and takes it very seriously. Zendaya tries to inform her fans in a positive way with her posts and pictures. She also knows that everything she does in the public eye makes a statement of some kind. Her behavior, the roles she takes, the music she makes, her clothing choices—and even her hairstyles—have the power to influence young people around the globe.

I, Zendaya

The name "Zendaya"—pronounced zen-DAY-uh—means "to give thanks" in a native language of Zimbabwe. Zendaya dropped her last name when she was 12 years old because she "just thought it was cool, like Cher or Prince."

Voice of Change

Zendaya uses her social media platform to speak out on important issues. She tackles racism, bullying, beauty standards, body image, and other topics head on. She also uses her fame to raise awareness and money for people in need. And she encourages her fans and followers to find their power and use their voices to make change. In an interview in *Glamour*, Zendaya said, "You have to learn to appreciate yourself and the power you hold. Whatever is inside of you—your soul, your power—find it. See it. Respect it. Protect it. And use it."

Zendaya uses her voice at a charity event for the homeless in 2017.

" " She Said It " "

"As my social platforms grew, I realized that my voice was so much more important than I had originally thought. I think if every young person understood the power of their voice, things would be a lot different."
—Interview in *Glamour*, October 2017

Setting the Stage

Zendaya Maree Stoermer Coleman was born on September 1, 1996, in Oakland, California. Her mother, Claire Marie, and her father, Kazembe Ajamu, were both teachers. Her mother also worked as a stage manager at the California Shakespeare Theater. Zendaya comes from a big, happy family. Her father also has two sons and two daughters from a previous marriage. Zendaya calls her family her "support system."

Zendaya has a close relationship with her parents.

First Act

As a young child, Zendaya was extremely quiet and shy. In fact, she had to repeat kindergarten because she refused to talk to the other kids! Growing up, Zendaya was more interested in basketball, soccer, and running than fashion. Each summer, she went to the theater where her mother worked. She got to watch all the plays and fell in love with acting. Soon she began acting herself in school and community plays. Her first role was as a witch in Shakespeare's play *Macbeth*. At age eight, she joined a kids' dance group called Future Shock Oakland. She loved learning hip-hop, hula, and other dances.

A Model Child

Zendaya began her career as a fashion model for stores like Old Navy and Gymboree and landed several TV commercials. While watching other kids during an audition for a Kidz Bop music video, she realized she faced tough competition. So she attempted a front flip, stuck the landing, and got a part. She proved she was willing to risk everything to succeed.

Shake It Up

In 2009, 13-year-old Zendaya auditioned for a new show on the Disney Channel called *Shake It Up*. The show was about two friends who become dancers on a local TV show. Zendaya read for the role of CeCe Jones, a fearless, street-smart troublemaker. She stood out from the crowd, but she did not get the part.

Instead of CeCe Jones, Zendaya was offered the part of Raquel "Rocky" Blue—the other leading role on the show.

❝ She Said It ❞

"My character and I are a lot alike, we are both goodie-two-shoes of the bunch. We love school and we like to excel in school and we are both trying to do the right things and help our friends and just be good people."
—Interview in *Glitter* about playing Rocky, May 2011

Gone Hollywood

Zendaya took the part of Rocky Blue and moved to Los Angeles with her father. The move was really difficult for the middle schooler. She missed her dog Midnight that she'd had since she was eight years old. She missed shopping with her friends. But most of all, she missed her mom. Zendaya's mother stayed behind in Oakland, working two jobs to help support the family. She could only visit Zendaya occasionally, and she missed her daughter so much she kept the TV on the Disney Channel all the time just to have her in the house.

Outgoing Zendaya soon made new friends on the set of *Shake It Up*.

"She Said It"

"I kind of came from Oakland [to] L.A. Although they're close, they're completely different worlds. That change was hard for me. I didn't have very many friends. The only friends I had were the people that were on my set, Shake It Up. *It's tough, when you're moving from somewhere and not knowing anyone."*
—Interview in *Huffington Post*, May 2014

Living the Dream

Leaving home was hard, but Zendaya says she was ecstatic to be living her dream. She had been hooked on the Disney Channel since she was five years old. Now she had a show of her own and was on the path to superstardom. And she didn't have to go it alone. Zendaya soon found a new best friend—her costar Bella Thorne. The girls met at auditions for the show and had an instant connection. *Shake It Up* **premiered** on the Disney Channel on November 7, 2010. It was an instant hit, and the girls were overnight sensations.

Busy Besties

Bella Thorne and Zendaya spent most of their time together. They filmed *Shake It Up* and recorded songs for the show's **soundtrack**. They also starred in a Disney Channel film called *Frenemies*. It tells the stories of three pairs of friends who become enemies and then "besties" again. Zendaya plays the part of Halley Brandon and fights with Bella's character over a job at a publishing company. In real life, the girls were building a strong friendship—which still lasts today. They are close friends who often text and call each other.

Zendaya and Bella did everything together in the early days—even becoming superstars!

11

A Fairy Tale Come True

Zendaya was rocking the role of Rocky Blue and was ready to take on the music scene next. The talented singer—who calls herself a hip-hop/**R&B** girl at heart—launched her music career just a few months after her television **debut**. She released a single in May 2011 called "Swag It Out." Zendaya explains the title means to show off or behave in a confident way. It showed off the young singer's own talent and swag. It also inspired the name for Zendaya's fans: "Zswaggers."

Fern

In November 2011, Zendaya changed things up by taking on a new role as the voice of a fairy named Fern in an **animated** special on the Disney Channel called *Pixie Hollow Games*. The story follows tiny fairies who compete in a series of events, including teacup races and dragonfly waterskiing.

Zendaya said voice acting for the role of Fern was challenging, but she loved the new experience.

Swagging It Out

In August 2012, Zendaya had what she called an epic moment in her life—she **signed** with Disney's Hollywood Records. Suddenly, the 15-year-old was kicking off her own concert tour. The Swag It Out tour began in her hometown of Oakland and lasted for more than two years. Zendaya performed at music festivals and state fairs across North America, adding new songs to the show as she went along. She released the hit dance single "Replay" in July 2013. Her debut album followed two months later. *Zendaya* was an electric mix of pop and R&B that included the tracks "Love You Forever," "Scared," and "Fireflies."

The summer of 2013 was a busy time for Zendaya. She also released a book entitled *Between U and Me: How to Rock Your Tween Years with Style and Confidence*. In her book, she offers advice and answers questions from fans.

Beauty and a Beat

Zendaya also brought some swag to the dance floor. In 2013, she took part in the dance competition show *Dancing with the Stars*. At 16, Zendaya was the youngest celebrity to ever appear on the show. She spent three months training and performing with pro dancer Val Chmerkovskiy, who said he was inspired by her talent and work ethic. They hip-hopped, waltzed, and quickstepped all the way to the finale—but lost to country singer Kellie Pickler and her dance partner Derek Hough.

Dance Fight

Zendaya's dance partner, Val, had to get 14 stitches after she elbowed him in the head during a rehearsal!

Zendaya and Val danced to many popular songs, including "Love on Top" by Beyoncé and "Beauty and a Beat" by Justin Bieber and Nicki Minaj.

Shake It Off

The final episode of *Shake It Up* aired on November 10, 2013. After three seasons on the Disney Channel, Zendaya was not the same wide-eyed girl who had signed on to play Rocky Blue. The 17-year-old performer had gained confidence and learned a lot about herself. She said, "I didn't start feeling comfortable using my voice until after *Shake It Up* ended." Zendaya had found her power and was ready to move on.

Zendaya was sad that her TV show was ending but was excited to shake things up in new ways.

Undercover Girl

Zendaya was growing up and leaving Rocky Blue in the past. But she was not done with the Disney Channel just yet. The star returned to TV in a magical movie and another hit show—this time on her own terms.

Making Magic

Zendaya began taking control in the summer of 2014—at least on TV. She played the lead role of Zoey Stevens in the Disney Channel movie *Zapped*. Zoey is an average teenage girl with serious guy troubles. She discovers a magical app on her phone that allows her to control the boys in her life. Zendaya describes the film as "a cute story," but says that in real life she would rather have an app that can **teleport** her places, make her food, or do her hair!

The clothes Zoey wears in the movie *Zapped* reflect Zendaya's own fashion style, just a little more girlie.

Finding Her Voice

The Disney Channel wanted Zendaya back to make more magic. She was offered the lead role in a new sitcom called *Super Awesome Katy*. The outspoken actor met with Disney bosses and, according to Zendaya's father, she "broke all the rules." Zendaya asked to be a producer so she could help make important decisions about the show—a bold request for a young performer. She wanted the show's name and her character's personality to reflect Zendaya's image as a role model for girls. And she insisted that the show feature a family of color. To her surprise, Disney agreed. The show was renamed *K.C. Undercover*, and Zendaya signed on as the star.

Zendaya and her TV family brought some **diversity** to the Disney Channel.

66 She Said It 99

*"When I left Disney, there weren't any families of color on the channel. I thought that was a big reason why I wanted to come back. I think I've successfully made a show that not only allows for **representation** but sees girls in a powerful and strong position."*
—Interview in *Variety*, August 2017

17

On a Mission

K.C. Undercover premiered on the Disney Channel in January 2015. Zendaya starred as Katrina Charlotte "K.C." Cooper, a high school math and technology whiz with a black belt in karate. She and her family work for a secret spy agency. Zendaya wanted K.C. to be a normal, smart, strong, socially awkward girl who could kick butt. She did not want her to be a singer or dancer, though, because she wanted to show "there are other things that a girl can be."

Birthday Wish

Zendaya had just turned 18 a few months before her new series debuted. To celebrate, Zendaya hosted a charity fund-raiser to bring food and clean water to children in Haiti, Tanzania, and the Philippines. The campaign helped more than 150 kids.

Oscar Buzz

Zendaya walked her first major red carpet a month after her new series debuted. She appeared at the Academy Awards in a stunning white goddess gown. But it was her hair that made headlines that night. Zendaya wore long, flowing dreadlocks—a ropelike hairstyle traditionally worn by African-Americans. A host of the TV show *Fashion Police* made a racist comment about the style. Zendaya took to social media and fired back at "ignorant people who choose to judge others based on the curl of their hair." Her direct post went viral. She received an outpouring of support from people around the world—and a public apology from the host.

Zendaya's look at the Academy Awards inspired the creation of a Barbie doll. The special-edition doll features a white, off-the-shoulder gown and long dreadlocks just like Zendaya's.

High School Grad

Zendaya's parents were both teachers, and she says she probably would have become one, too, if she hadn't become an actor. Her busy schedule, beginning at such a young age, made it hard for her to stay in school. But she knew how important her own education was. Zendaya's father started homeschooling her when they moved to Los Angeles. She also had a teacher who worked with her on set, on the road, and everywhere else the busy performer went. It wasn't easy, but her hard work paid off. Zendaya graduated from Oak Park High School in June 2015.

Zendaya's father supported her dreams, but he also made sure she got an education.

She Said It

"Graduating high school ... is really inspiring to a lot of kids my age who might be having trouble getting through high school. Hopefully, I'm showing people that if I can do it, they can do it."
—Interview in *Galore*, September 2015

In Their Shoes

Zendaya's parents taught her more than just the value of an education. She has said, "My mom is like a **shero**. My dad is so strong." Zendaya also admires former US First Lady Michelle Obama; singers Beyoncé, Rihanna, and Michael Jackson; and television producer Shonda Rhimes. But mostly, she confesses to being "obsessed" with Oprah Winfrey, a former talk show host and successful media **entrepreneur**.

Picture Perfect

Zendaya's natural beauty caught the attention of CoverGirl, which made her the newest face of the cosmetics company in 2016. Staff there admired her for being "unapologetically herself." Nowhere is this more true than on photo shoots. After posing for *Modeliste* magazine, Zendaya was shocked to see that her waist and thighs had been slimmed down and her skin had been bronzed in the photos. She spoke out about it on Instagram, posting a real picture beside a **retouched** picture. The magazine pulled the issue and published the original photos instead.

Zendaya wants to follow Oprah Winfrey's example as a creative person with a good head for business.

One Fine Daya

Known for making bold statements, Zendaya describes her personal style as "fearless." Inspired by the clothes worn by regular, everyday people, Zendaya launched her own collection, called Daya by Zendaya, in 2016. The collection has grown from shoes, such as **stilettos** and ballet flats, to clothing, such as street-style jumpsuits, hoodies, and joggers. The always inclusive and body-positive Zendaya had three requirements for her clothes: they had to be affordable, come in a wide range of sizes, and be something both females and males could wear.

Zendaya has said that she wants women to feel fearless when they wear her shoes.

Dating Undercover

Zendaya is a social media star who loves to engage with her fans on Twitter, Instagram, and Snapchat. She often posts behind-the-scenes pictures and videos with her family and friends—including her niece Ezenia "Zink" Coleman. But Zendaya keeps her dating life undercover. She confessed in 2016 that she once had a secret boyfriend for four years who broke her heart. She was also rumored to have dated pro football player Odell Beckham Jr.

Taking on Spider-Man

In the summer of 2017, Zendaya made her feature film debut, appearing in the blockbuster hit *Spider-Man: Homecoming*. Zendaya plays the **iconic** comic-book character M.J. Jones—a smart, sarcastic bookworm who goes to the same school as Peter Parker (aka Spider-Man). The superhero film was a smash hit—and Zendaya became a real-life movie star. Since then, she has been linked to *Spider-Man* star Tom Holland, but Zendaya insists they are just friends.

Award Season

Zendaya won a Teen Choice Award for her role in the *Spider-Man* movie. In fact, people have been singing her praises ever since she started performing. Zendaya has been nominated for and won many Kids and Teen Choice Awards for her roles in Disney shows and movies, her music and videos, her style, and even her tweets on Twitter!

Zendaya owned the red carpet at the premiere of *Spider-Man: Homecoming*.

66 She Said It 99

"It was nice to play a character who wasn't a damsel in distress, but actually very smart, quirky, different and outspoken."
—On her role as M.J. in *Spider-Man: Homecoming*, *Variety*, August 2017

Zendaya Soars

The third season of *K.C. Undercover* premiered in the summer of 2017. The spy show was as popular as ever, but all good things must come to an end. Zendaya revealed this would be the final season of the Disney sitcom. She took to Twitter to make the announcement—peppered with lots of crying emojis. Zendaya grew up on the Disney Channel and was sad to say goodbye. But it was time for the multitalented star to look to the future.

Zendaya strikes a pose and shows off her fierce fashion sense on the red carpet.

Singing to Her Own Beat

Zendaya's fans had been eagerly waiting for her second album. She was signed by Republic Records and released a single called "Something New" featuring Chris Brown in 2016. Zendaya wanted to make a new wave R&B album, but the **label** wanted pop songs. She refused to give in, and although she hopes one day to finish the album, she is focusing on her acting career.

24

Fearless Zendaya flies high in *The Greatest Showman*.

Fly Girl

Zendaya's second feature film opened in theaters in December 2017. *The Greatest Showman* is a musical drama about P.T. Barnum—played by Hugh Jackman—and how he started his famous circus. Zendaya plays the part of a pink-haired trapeze artist named Anne Wheeler. The fearless actor insisted on doing all her own high-flying stunts, even though she admits it was extremely scary. She steals former Disney star Zac Efron's heart in the movie. Sparks fly when they sing a duet called "Rewrite the Stars"—which once again sparked dating rumors! But the pair insists that they are just "great partners."

" He Said It "

"She's what I call a unicorn. I don't know if there has been anyone like Zendaya or will be anyone ever again. That girl makes it all look absolutely effortless."
—Hugh Jackman in *Entertainment Weekly*, August 2017

Her Biggest Role

Zendaya continues to play an important part both on and off the screen—as a role model for people everywhere. The influential star believes she does a world of good just by being herself. She calls herself a *real* model instead of a *role* model. She says, "I'm not pretending to be some good kid that's perfect. It just happens that I'm a good kid, and I don't do bad stuff and I like to be positive because that's just how I was raised." Zendaya has led national discussions on issues, including race, bullying, and gender, with a positive attitude and "knowledge in her voice."

At the InStyle awards in October 2017, Zendaya wore her hair in an **Afro** as a tribute to her aunts who fought in the civil rights movement. The hairstyle was worn by her "aunties" in the 1960s and 1970s.

A World of Good

Zendaya has always known the importance of helping others. When she was eight years old, she asked her friends to donate to an animal shelter instead of buying her birthday gifts. Today, she uses her fame to raise awareness and help people all around the world. Each year, Zendaya asks her followers to donate to a charity. She has raised money for siblings in South Africa who lost their parents to **AIDS**, helped women in poor communities start their own businesses, and provided disaster relief to victims of Hurricane Harvey in Texas. Zendaya has also worked with a number of charities, including Convoy of Hope and Friends for Change, that support education, health, and human and animal rights.

Zendaya and singer Mary J. Blige are pretty in pink at a fundraising event.

66 She Said It 99

"[Acting] has been my passion. But as I've started to understand the power and influence I have, I've realized it's really this avenue for me to do bigger, more meaningful things. For me to help somebody."
—Interview in *Glamour*, November 2016

Stay Tuned

Being identified as a Disney child star can sometimes make it difficult for actors to move into adult acting roles. But as Zendaya has grown up, fans have eagerly followed. Right now, she is focusing on acting and looks forward to one day producing and creating her own TV shows and films. And if what she's working on doesn't make her happy, this actor, singer, dancer, style entrepreneur, and activist will move on to something that does. That's the beauty of being the multitalented Zendaya!

"She Said It"

"I don't just sing, dance, and act because I love it. You have to have a purpose, and mine is to connect with the world, to get across messages that are important. I'd much rather be known for leaving a little stamp of positivity on one person's life than for the last project that I did."

—Interview in *Glamour*, February 2016

Timeline

1996: Zendaya Maree Stoermer Coleman is born in Oakland, California on September 1

2009: She lands a leading role on a new sitcom on the Disney Channel

2010: *Shake It Up* premieres and is an instant hit

2011: Zendaya releases a single called "Swag It Out"

2011: She and Bella Thorne release a duet called "Watch Me"

2011: Zendaya voices the character Fern in the *Pixie Hollow Games*

2012: She stars in the Disney Channel movie *Frenemies*

2012: The Swag It Out tour kicks off in Oakland

2012: She signs with Disney's Hollywood Records

2013: Zendaya competes on the TV show *Dancing with the Stars*

2013: Zendaya's dance single "Replay" is released

2013: Her book, *Between U and Me: How to Rock Your Tween Years with Style and Confidence*, is published

2013: Her debut album, *Zendaya*, is released

2014: She stars in the Disney Channel movie *Zapped*

2015: *K.C. Undercover* premieres on the Disney Channel with Zendaya as a coproducer and the star of the show

2015: Zendaya graduates from high school

2016: She becomes the newest face of CoverGirl

2016: She releases a single called "Something New" featuring Chris Brown

2016: She launches her fashion line, Daya by Zendaya

2017: Zendaya appears in her first feature film, *Spider-Man: Homecoming*

2017: Her second feature film, *The Greatest Showman*, opens in theaters

2019: Zendaya is expected to appear in the sequel to *Spider-Man: Homecoming*

Glossary

activist A person who uses or supports strong actions to help make changes in society

Afro A hairstyle of tight curls in a full rounded shape that was popular in the African-American community in the late 1960s

AIDS A serious disease of the immune system that is caused by a virus

animated Made in the form of a cartoon

debut To first appear or to be performed in public for the first time

diversity Including people who are different races or have different cultures

entrepreneur A person who starts a business and takes risks to make money

iconic Very famous or popular

label A company that makes and sells recorded music

outspoken Direct and open in speech

premiere To be shown in public for the first time

R&B Rhythm and blues, a form of popular African-American music

representation A person or group that speaks for or acts in support of another person or group

retouch To make changes to a photo to make it look better

role model Someone who shows others how to behave well

shero A female hero

signed Hired by a record company or other type of company

soundtrack A recording made up of songs from a TV show or movie

stiletto A woman's shoe with a narrow high heel

teleport To move from one place to another instantly without crossing the space between them, usually in science fiction

Find Out More

Books

Caravantes, Peggy. *Zendaya: Star Performer*. Big Buddy Biographies. Momentum, 2017.

Lajiness, Katie. *Zendaya: Famous Entertainer*. Big Buddy Books, 2017.

Zendaya. *Between U and Me: How to Rock Your Tween Years with Style and Confidence*. Disney-Hyperion, 2013.

Websites

Visit Zendaya's official website for music, photos, videos, beauty and style tips, recipes, charity projects, and more: https://zendaya.com

Visit the Disney Channel website to play a fun *K.C. Undercover* spy game: www.disneychannel.ca/games/k-c-undercover-robo-recon

Social Media

Read Zendaya's award-winning tweets on her Twitter feed: https://twitter.com/Zendaya

Join the 49 million people who follow Zendaya on Instagram: www.instagram.com/zendaya

Index

About the Author

Robin Johnson is a freelance author and editor who has written more than 75 children's books. When she isn't working, Robin enjoys traveling, feeding her sock monkey obsession, and trying to outwit her husband and teenage sons in strategy games.

32